The HUNT

Narelle Oliver

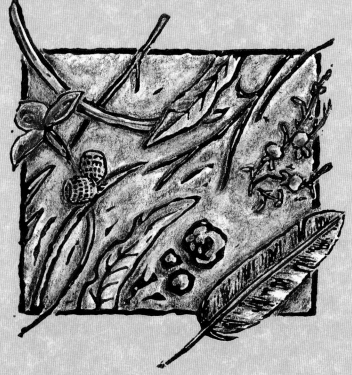

*There is something magical about suddenly seeing something
that to most passers-by is invisible. The sheer cunning of the myriad
of disguises honed by natural selection is a source of great intellectual joy
and a child-like sense of awe* — Paul Zborowski, Entomologist.

A Lothian Book

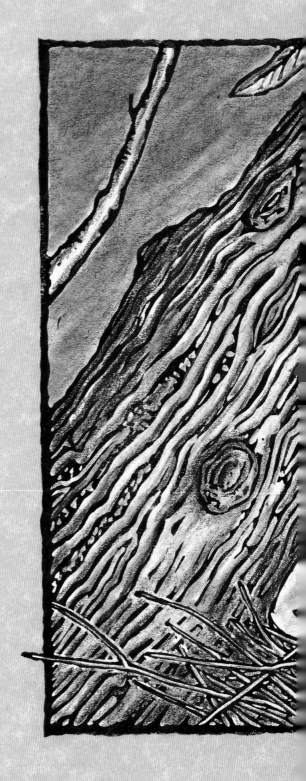

Harsh cries of hunger
pierce the chill air.

Twilight is fading.

The Tawny Frogmouth's
hunt must begin.

On silent wings, the frogmouth flies...
watching for a flicker of movement,
listening for the faintest sound.

4

At that moment
a Bark Moth flutters towards a tree.

Before the frogmouth can snap it up,
the moth has disappeared.

Nearby
a Bush Cricket hops from leaf to leaf.

The frogmouth follows, but in a flash,
the Bush Cricket has vanished.

Just then
a Retiarius Spider swings down
across the breeze.

In an instant
the spider is somewhere out of sight.

Meanwhile
a Brown Leaf Moth skims across the ground.

Only a second later
there is no sign of it.

Out from the leaves
a stripy Tree Frog long-jumps into view.

All of a sudden
the stripy frog is nowhere to be found.

Close by
a Leaf-tail Gecko scuttles up a granite rock.

15

In the twinkling of an eye
there is no trace of it at all.

Like an arrow
a Stick Insect shoots to a branch above.

In the very next moment
the Stick Insect has gone.

Finally, an Emperor Gum Moth drifts down
through the She-oak twigs.

19

This time there is no escape

and it seems the hunt is won.

But overhead, a Powerful Owl is watching.

Sensing danger, the frogmouth swoops
to land.

Now the frogmouth has disappeared

so the Powerful Owl flies on.

The frogmouth waits,
silent and still.

Then noiseless wing beats
take the hunter home.

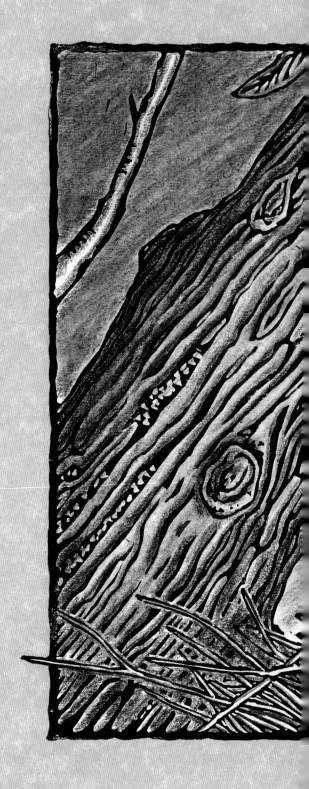

Can you find all the camouflaged creatures?

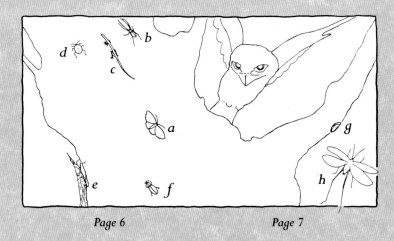

Page 6   Page 7

CAMOUFLAGED
a Bark Moth (*Ectropis subtinctaria*)
Wingspan: 45 mm
(appears uncamouflaged on page 5)
b Crab Spider (*Stephanopis cambridgei*)
Body length: 12 mm
c Cream-striped Shinning-skink (*Cryptoblepharus virgatus*)
Full length: 90 mm
d Shield Bug nymph (Family: Pentatomidae)
Length: 15 mm
e Grasshopper (Genus: *Coryphistes*)
Length: 80 mm
f Diamond Beetle (*Chrysolopus spectabilis*)
Length: 20 mm
g Tree-hopper nymph (Genus: *Ledromorpha*)
Length: 15 mm
NOT CAMOUFLAGED
h Bush Cricket (*Caedicia olivacea*)
Length: 55 mm

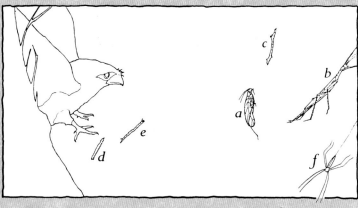

Page 8   Page 9

CAMOUFLAGED
a Bush Cricket (*Caedicia olivacea*)
Length: 55 mm
(appears uncamouflaged on page 7)
b Ringbarker Phasmatid or Stick Insect (*Podacanthus wilkinsoni*)
Length: 110 mm
c Twisted Moth caterpillar (*Circopetes obtusata*)
Length: 60 mm
d Triangular Moth caterpillar (*Epidesmia chilonaria*)
Length: 40 mm
e Gum Snout Moth caterpillar (*Entometa fervens*)
Length: 60 mm
NOT CAMOUFLAGED
f Retiarius Spider (*Dinopis subrufa*)
Body length: 23 mm

Page 10   Page 11

CAMOUFLAGED
a Retiarius Spider (*Dinopis subrufa*)
Body length: 23 mm
(appears uncamouflaged on page 9)
b Grass-mimicking Phasmatid or Stick Insect
(Genus: *Sipyloidea*)
Length: 100 mm
c Flower Spider (*Diaea rosea*)
Body length: 6 mm
d Black Geometrid Moth (*Melanodes anthracitaria*)
Wingspan: 40 mm
e Black Praying Mantis* (Genus: *Paraoxypilus*)
Length: 25 mm
f Crab Spider* (*Stephanopis scabra*)
Body length: 9 mm
g Bark-hopping Bug* (Family: *Eurybrachyidae*)
Length: 8 mm
NOT CAMOUFLAGED
h Brown Leaf Moth (*Phallaria ophiusaria*)
Wingspan: 60 mm
* These species have developed black colouration for
camouflage on trees and logs blackened by bushfires.

CAMOUFLAGED

a Brown Leaf Moth (*Phallaria ophiusaria*)
Wingspan: 60 mm
(appears uncamouflaged on page 11)
b Twisted Moth (*Circopetes obtusata*)
Wingspan: 55 mm
c Copper-tailed Ctenotus ('ten-oh'-tus) (*Ctenotus taeniolatus*)
Full length: 170 mm
d Striped Marsh Frog (*Limnodynastes peronii*)
Body length: 65 mm
e Delicate Mouse (*Pseudomys delicatulus*)
Full length: 150 mm

NOT CAMOUFLAGED

f Verreaux's Tree Frog (*Litoria verreauxii*)
Body length: 30 mm

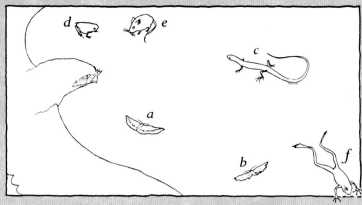

Page 12   *Page 13*

CAMOUFLAGED

a Verreaux's Tree Frog (*Litoria verreauxii*)
Body length: 30 mm
(appears uncamouflaged on page 13)
b Praying Mantid (Family: *Mantidae*)
Length: 60 mm
c Long-horned Grasshopper (Genus: *Caedicia*)
Length: 40 mm
d Phasmatid or Stick Insect (Genus: *Tropididerus*)
Length: 100 mm
e Barking Marsh Frog (*Limnodynastes fletcheri*)
Body length: 50 mm
f Evening Brown Butterfly caterpillar (*Melanitis leda*)
Length: 35 mm

NOT CAMOUFLAGED

g Rough-throated Leaf-tail Gecko (*Phyllurus salebrosus*)
Full length: 160 mm

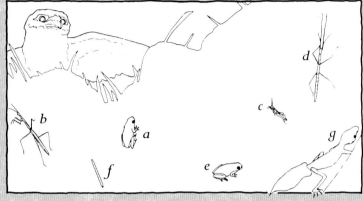

Page 14   *Page 15*

CAMOUFLAGED

a Rough-throated Leaf-tail Gecko (*Phyllurus salebrosus*)
Full length: 160 mm
(appears uncamouflaged on page 15)
b Grey Huntsman Spider (Genus: *Holconia*)
Span: 90 mm
c Brown Huntsman Spider (Genus: *Heteropoda*)
Span: 70 mm
d Geometrid Moth (*Pingasa calliglauca*)
Wingspan: 35 mm
e Geometrid Moth (*Anisozyga pieroides*)
Wingspan: 35 mm

NOT CAMOUFLAGED

f Phasmatid or Stick Insect (*Xeroderus kirbii*)
Length: 100 mm

Page 16   *Page 17*

CAMOUFLAGED

a Phasmatid or Stick Insect (*Xeroderus kirbii*)
Length: 100 mm
(appears uncamouflaged on page 17)
b Retiarius Spider (Dinopis bicornis)
Body length: 20 mm
c Bird-dropping Spider (*Calaenia kinbergi*)
Body length: 12 mm
d Casuarina Moth caterpillar (*Brachyptila vitulina*)
Length: 60 mm
e Ootheca (egg case) of Praying Mantid (Family: Mantidae)
Length: 25 mm
f Tree gall created by Casuarina Gall-making Bug*
(Genus: *Cylindrococcus*)
Length: 15 mm

NOT CAMOUFLAGED

g Emperor Gum Moth (*Opodiphthera eucalypti*)
Wingspan: 130 mm

* *At the place where the bug burrows into the tree, a gall
is formed which looks like the tree's cones. Therefore
the bug's entry point is diguised.*

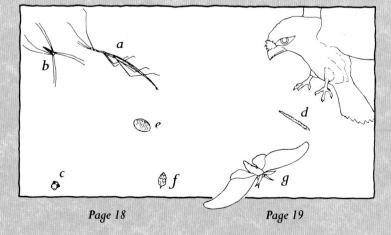

Page 18   *Page 19*

The Setting of this Story

The Hunt is set in the granite-belt country of south-east Queensland, Australia. It is a place of dramatic granite expanses, precariously balanced boulders, wildflowers, gnarled eucalypts and she-oaks. The dominance of the speckled granite rock, along with more common background textures of leaves, leaf litter, twigs, grasses and tree bark, suggested exciting possibilities for the setting of a story based on the trickery of camouflage and disguise. These possibilities were confirmed when I joined Patrick Couper (Curator, Vertebrates, at the Queensland Museum) on a nocturnal creature-spotting expedition at Girraween National Park. The expedition yielded a number of Leaf-tail Geckoes, other geckoes, spiders, frogs and moths so perfectly camouflaged on their granite backgrounds that, even when the rocks were ablaze with torchlight, we were often only able to locate them by focusing on their eyeshine.

Crypsis: The Trickery of Camouflage and Disguise

To survive on this planet, many animals must find ways to hide from their predators (those animals which will eat them), or to hide while they are stalking their own prey. One particularly fascinating way of hiding developed by a number of animals is that of 'crypsis'. 'Crypsis' works in two different ways: camouflage and disguise.

Camouflage

Animals which use the camouflage technique blend in with their backgrounds through their colour, patterning and tone. The Bark Moth and Leaf-tail Gecko are two creatures which use this technique. Often the animal's patterning breaks up its shape and outline. This can be through a random arrangement of colours or through a strong stripe or pattern which divides the animal's body shape into smaller, unrecognisable shapes. According to many studies, predators of insects memorise the shape of their favourite prey, and this becomes their 'search image'. However, if an insect's general shape is broken up by a strong pattern, it will not be associated with its predator's search image. (Zborowski, 1991, p.6)

To become really invisible, some of these animals use extra tricks; for example, some appear flat or two-dimensional on their backgrounds. This is achieved through 'counter-shading'. In normal circumstances an uncamouflaged animal will appear three-dimensional (and therefore stick out from its background) because its lower sides will be in shadow (therefore appearing darker), while its upper middle section will be in sunlight (so appearing lighter). When a camouflaged animal is counter-shaded, its own colouring is darker on its upper middle section and lighter on its lower sides. This cancels out the effects of normal 'shading' on the animal, and thus flattens its appearance. Many frogs are shaded in this way.

Even if an animal is well camouflaged through its colour, patterning and the trick of counter-shading, it may still be visible because it is casting a shadow. To overcome this problem, some animals, such as certain butterflies, lean over so that their shadow is reduced. Other insects align themselves with the direction of the sunlight, and some creatures have a special flange-shaped edge which blends smoothly with the surface they are resting on, so no shadow is created. The Bark Moth has such a flanged edge on its wings.

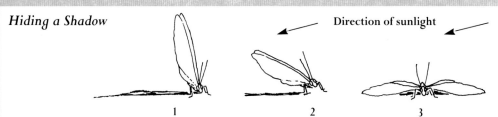

Hiding a Shadow   Direction of sunlight

1   2   3

1 With wings upright, this butterfly casts a large, long, lateral shadow.
2 Leaning over, the shadow is reduced and mostly obscured by the wings.
3 When the flanged edges of the wings merge with the surroundings, the shadow is completely hidden.

Disguise

Animals which use the disguise technique have developed features that help them to resemble an object (usually inedible) in their environment. In other words, they are 'dressed up' to look like something else, such as a leaf or a twig, which will not interest their predators. The Brown Leaf Moth and the Stick Insect use this disguise trick.

Behaviour

Of course, none of these tricks of camouflage and disguise work unless the animals behave in a certain way. In most cases they need to keep still, and they often need the correct posture. The Tawny Frogmouth, for example, is only disguised as a broken branch when it strikes a stiff, elongated pose. Some creatures use particular movements. Praying Mantids rock like foliage swaying in the breeze, while Stick Insects, if disturbed, may drop to the ground and lie still like broken twigs.

Although the distinction between camouflage and disguise is a useful one, there are many animals which rely on both techniques. The Bush Cricket, for example, merges with a green leaf through its colour and the pattern of veins on its wings, but its overall shape is also rather like a single leaf.

ACKNOWLEDGEMENTS

'The study of camouflage is a slippery combination of science, experience and blind fortuitous luck' (Paul Zborowski). For their very generous assistance with my own 'slippery' crypsis research, I wish to thank: Patrick Couper, Curator, Vertebrates, Queensland Museum; Rose and Ben Komdüur (for access to and information about the Tawny Frogmouths living on their property); Phillip Lawless, Assistant Curator, Arachnology, Queensland Museum; Geoff Monteith, Senior Curator, Lower Entomology, Queensland Museum; Rae Sheridan, Education Officer, Queensland Museum; and Geoff Thompson, Senior Technician, Lower Entomology, Queensland Museum.

BIBLIOGRAPHY

Bomford, L., *Camouflage and Colour*, Boxtree, London, 1992.

Brackenbury, J., *Insects in Flight*, Blandford, UK, 1992.

Coupar, P. & M., *Flying Colours: Common Caterpillars, Butterflies and Moths of South-Eastern Australia*, NSW University Press, Sydney, 1992.

Dahms, E., Monteith, G. & Monteith, S., *Collecting, Preserving and Classifying Insects*, Queensland Museum, Brisbane, 1979.

Dale, F., *Forty Queensland Lizards*, Queensland Museum, Brisbane, 1973.

Davies, V., *Australian Spiders: Collection, Preservation and Identification*, Queensland Museum, Brisbane, 1986.

Ehmann, H., The Australian Museum & The National Photographic Index of Australian Wildlife, *Encyclopedia of Australian Animals: Reptiles*, (Series Editor: Ronald Strahan), Collins Angus & Robertson, Sydney, 1992.

Fogden, M. & P., *Animals and their Colour*, Eurobook, London, 1974.

Hadlington, P. & Johnston, J., *An Introduction to Australian Insects*, NSW University Press, Sydney, 1988.

Harvey, M. & Yen, A., *Worms to Wasps: An Illustrated Guide to Australia's Terrestrial Invertebrates*, Oxford University Press, Melbourne, 1989.

Hollands, D., *Birds of the Night: Owls, Frogmouths and Nightjars of Australia*, Reed, Sydney, 1991.

Mascord, R., *Australian Spiders in Colour*, Reed, Sydney, 1970.

Readers Digest Complete Book of Australian Birds, 2nd edn, Reader's Digest Services, Sydney, 1986.

Robinson, M., *A Field Guide to Frogs of Australia*, Australian Museum/Reed, Sydney, 1993.

Scott, H., *Historical Drawings of Moths and Butterflies: From the Collections of the Australian Museum*, The Craftsman House, Roseville, 1988.

Simpson, K. (ed.) & Day, N. (illus.), *Field Guide to the Birds of Australia*, Penguin, Sydney, 1993.

Strahan, R. (ed.), *The Australian Museum Complete Book of Australian Mammals*, Angus & Robertson, Sydney, 1983.

Walker, E., *Granite Wilderness*, International Colour Productions, Stanthorpe, 1982.

Zborowski, P., *Animals in Disguise*, Reed, Sydney, 1991.

For my parents, who introduced me to
the spectacular landscape of Girraween National Park
some thirty years ago.

For Greg, who showed me other ways of seeing it.

A Lothian Book

Thomas C. Lothian Pty Ltd
11 Munro Street, Port Melbourne, Victoria 3207

Copyright © Narelle Oliver 1995
First published 1995

National Library of Australia
Cataloguing-in-publication data:
Oliver, Narelle, 1960 -
The hunt.
ISBN 0 85091 707 7.
1. Animals - Australia - Juvenile literature.
2. Podargidae - Australia - Juvenile literature. I. Title.
598.99

Illustration media: linocuts hand-coloured with
coloured pencils and pastels
Designed by Lynn Twelftree
Typeset in Perpetua Bold
Printed in Hong Kong by Colorcraft Ltd